FAITH

FAITH

Edited by
Benjamin Unseth

GARBORG'S Inc.

Bloomington, MN 55431

Faith, The Little Books of Virtue, Series One

Edited by Benjamin Unseth

Copyright © 1995 by Garborg's, Inc.
P. O. Box 20132, Bloomington, MN 55420

ISBN 1-881830-21-7

The world is a great sculptor's shop.

We are the statues and there is a rumor going

round the shop that some of us are some day

going to come to life.

C. S. LEWIS

FAITH

There are no tricks in plain and simple faith.

SHAKESPEARE

Faith, mighty faith, the promise sees,

And looks to God alone;

Laughs at impossibilities,

And cries it shall be done.

CHARLES WESLEY

MAN IS WHAT HE BELIEVES.

ANTON CHEKHOV

At Ravensbruck, a Nazi concentration camp where more than 90,000 women and children died, this prayer was found on a piece of wrapping paper near a child's corpse:

O Lord, remember not only the men and women of good will, but also those of ill will. But do not only remember all the suffering they have inflicted on us, remember the fruits we bought, thanks to this

suffering: our comradeship, our loyalty, our humility,

the courage, the generosity, the greatness of heart

which has grown out of all this. And when they come

to judgment, let all the fruits that we have borne be

their forgiveness. ❖

ut even so, you love me!

You are holding my right hand!

You will keep on guiding me all my life with your
    wisdom and counsel;
    and afterwards receive me into the glories
        of heaven!

Whom have I in heaven but you?

And I desire no one on earth as much as you!

My health fails; my spirits droop, yet God remains!

He is the strength of my heart....

As for me, I get as close to him as I can!

I have chosen him and I will tell everyone about
    the wonderful ways he rescues me. ✿

PSALM 73:23-28 TLB

FAITH

Faith is the force of life.

LEO TOLSTOY

For faith is the beginning and the
end is love, and God is the two of
them brought into unity.

ST. IGNATIUS

A perfect faith would lift us
absolutely above fear.

GEORGE MacDONALD

Faith is required of thee, and a sincere
life, not loftiness of intellect, nor deepness
in the mysteries of God.

THOMAS À KEMPIS

We trust not because "a God" exists,
but because *this* God exists.

C. S. LEWIS

Nothing in life is more
wonderful than faith—
the one great moving force
which we can neither weigh
in the balance nor test in
the crucible.

SIR WILLIAM OSLER

THOMAS A. DORSEY

Precious Lord, take my hand,

Lead me on, help me stand —

I am tired, I am weak, I am worn;

Through the storm, through the night,

Lead me on to the light —

Take my hand, precious Lord,

lead me home.

When my way grows drear,

Precious Lord, linger near—

When my life is almost gone;

Hear my cry, hear my call,

Hold my hand lest I fall—

Lead me home.

Take my hand, precious Lord,

lead me home. ✿

You need not seek Him here or there:

He is no farther off than the door of

the heart. There He stands and waits,

and waits until He finds you ready to

open and let Him in. Your opening

and His entering are but one moment.

MEISTER ECKHART

FAITH

12

LET US HAVE FAITH THAT
RIGHT MAKES MIGHT,
AND IN THAT FAITH LET
US TO THE END DARE TO
DO OUR DUTY AS WE
UNDERSTAND IT.

ABRAHAM LINCOLN

FAITH
13

PSALM 86:10-13 TLB

Y ou are great, and do great miracles.

You alone are God.

Tell me where you want me to go

and I will go there.

May every fiber of my being unite

in reverence to your name.

With all my heart I will praise you.

I will give glory to your name forever,

for you love me so much!

You are constantly so kind!

WILLIAM COWPER

God moves in a mysterious way

His wonders to perform;

He plants His footsteps in the sea,

And rides upon the storm.

BROTHER LAWRENCE

en invent means and methods of coming

at God's love; they learn rules and set up

devices to remind them of that love, and

it seems like a world of trouble to bring

oneself into the consciousness of God's

presence. Yet it might be so simple. Is it

not quicker and easier just to do our

common business wholly for the love of Him? Thus we put His consecration upon all we lay our hands to, at the same time establishing communion of our hearts with His, summoning the sense of His abiding presence. There is need of neither art nor science. We go, as we are, to Him, unpretending, single-hearted. ❀

True religion is not the separable accident of a life; it is that which runs through and animates and pervades the life. It is not the altar set up within the house; it is the loving inspiration which breathes through the house. It consists not so much in external works of piety as in the habit of carrying all the restraints and sanctities of godliness into the transactions of everyday life, making conscience of our gains, prescribing rules for our pleasures, imposing limits upon our self-expenditure, helping, doing good upon a principle and upon a plan—in a word, in everything we undertake to do or purpose, having regard to an unseen but ever-controlling Presence. ❀

GEORGE MUELLER

A VOICE IS IN THE WIND
I DO NOT KNOW;
A MEANING ON THE FACE
OF THE HIGH HILLS
WHOSE UTTERANCE
I CANNOT COMPREHEND.
A SOMETHING IS BEHIND THEM:
THAT IS GOD.

GEORGE MACDONALD

FAITH

O Love that will not let me go,

I rest my weary soul in Thee;

I give Thee back the life I owe,

That in Thine ocean depths its flow

May richer, fuller be.

O Joy that seekest me through pain,

I cannot close my heart to Thee;

I trace the rainbow through the rain,

And feel the promise is not vain

That morn shall tearless be.

GEORGE MATHESON

He, who from zone to zone

Guides through the boundless sky

thy certain flight,

In the long way that I must tread alone,

Will lead my steps aright.

WILLIAM CULLEN BRYANT
To a Waterfowl

God will never, never, never let us down if we have faith and put our trust in Him. He will always look after us. So we must cleave to Jesus. Our whole life must simply be woven into Jesus.

MOTHER TERESA
Awarded Nobel prize for peace, 1979

Strong Son of God, Immortal Love,

Whom we, that have not seen thy face,

By faith, and faith alone, embrace.

ALFRED, LORD TENNYSON

I never saw a moor,

I never saw the sea;

Yet know I how the heather looks,

And what a wave must be.

I never spoke with God,

Nor visited in heaven;

Yet certain am I of the spot

As if the chart were given.

EMILY DICKINSON

IT IS BY FAITH YOU STAND FIRM.

2 CORINTHIANS 1:24 NIV

G.K. CHESTERTON

I had always believed that the world involved magic: now I thought perhaps it involved a magician. And this pointed a profound emotion always present and sub-conscious; that this world of ours has some purpose; and if there is a purpose, there is a person. I had always felt life first as a story: and if there is a story there is a story-teller. ❁

JAMES T. FIELDS
The Tempest

We were crowded in the cabin,

    Not a soul would dare to sleep,—

It was midnight on the water

    And a storm was on the deep.

'Tis a fearful thing in winter

    To be shattered by the blast,

And to hear the rattling trumpet

    Thunder, "Cut away the mast!"

So we shuddered there in silence,—

    For the stoutest held his breath,

While the hungry sea was roaring,

    And the breakers talked with Death.

As thus we sat in darkness,

    Each one busy in his prayers,

"We are lost!" the captain shouted

    As he staggered down the stairs.

But his little daughter whispered,

As she took his icy hand,

"Isn't God upon the ocean

Just the same as on the land?"

Then we kissed the little maiden,

And we spoke in better cheer,

And we anchored safe in harbor

When the morn was shining clear. ❀

Far away, there in the sunshine, are my highest aspirations. I may not reach them, but I can look up and see their beauty, believe in them, and try to follow where they lead.

LOUISA MAY ALCOTT

Alone I walked the ocean strand;

A pearly shell was in my hand:

I stooped and wrote upon the sand

    My name—the year—the day.

As onward from the spot I passed,

One lingering look behind I cast;

A wave came rolling high and fast,

    And washed my lines away.

And so, me thought, 'twill shortly be

With every mark on earth from men

A wave of dark oblivion's sea

    Will sweep across the place

Where I have trod the sandy shore

Of time, and been, to be no more,

Of me—my day—the name I bore,

    To leave nor track nor trace.

And yet, with Him who counts the sands

And holds the waters in His hands,

I know a lasting record stands

 Inscribed against my name,

Of all this mortal part has wrought,

Of all this thinking soul has thought,

And from these fleeting moments caught

 For glory or for shame.

HANNAH FLAGG GOULD
A Name in the Sand

Faith is...

Faith is the first factor in a life devoted to
service. Without faith, nothing is possible.
With it, nothing is impossible.

MARY McLEOD BETHUNE

Faith is a kind of winged intellect. The
great workmen of history have been men
who believed like giants.

DR. CHARLES H. PARKHURST

Faith is like a lily, lifted high and white.

CHRISTINA ROSSETTI

GOD'S IN HIS HEAVEN— ALL'S RIGHT WITH THE WORLD!

ROBERT BROWNING

MARTIN LUTHER KING, JR.

I have a dream that one day every valley

Ûhall be exalted, every hill and mountain shall be

made low, the rough places will be made plain,

and the crooked places will be made straight, and

the glory of the Lord shall be revealed, and all

flesh shall see it together.

This is our hope. This is the faith with which

I return to the South. With this faith we will be

able to hew out of the mountain of despair a stone

of hope. With this faith we will be able to

transform the jangling discords of our nation

into a beautiful symphony of brotherhood.

With this faith we will be able to work

together, to pray together, to struggle together,

to go to jail together, to stand up for freedom

together, knowing that we'll be free one day.

spoken to more than 200,000 people in Washington D.C. on
August 28, 1963

FAITH

37

Blossoms are scattered by the wind and the wind cares nothing, but the blossoms of the heart no wind can touch.

YOSHIDA KENKO

RUTH STAFFORD PEALE

The Reverend Norman Vincent Peale speaking to President Chiang Kai-shek of China:

"Mr. President," Norman says, "you amaze me. Despite your age you still have a clear eye, great vigor, unwrinkled skin, perfect health. You just don't seem to grow old. How do you do it?"

The Generalissimo smiles. "It's simple," he tells us. "I pray three times a day!"

Madame Chiang translates this for us. Then she adds, "He says he prays three times a day. What he means is that he devotes himself to prayer and meditation for thirty minutes three times a day. No one is allowed to interrupt or disturb him during these periods for any reason whatsoever." ✿

Washington never could have

succeeded except for the aid of Divine providence,

upon which he at all times relied. I feel that I

cannot succeed without the same Divine aid

which sustained him; and in the same Almighty

Being I place my reliance for support; and I hope

you, my friends, will all pray that I may receive

that Divine assistance, without which I cannot

succeed, but with which success is certain. Again

I bid you all an affectionate farewell. ❁

ABRAHAM LINCOLN

from his farewell as he departed Springfield, Illinois for Washington D.C.

FAITH

41

The meaning of earthly existence is not, as we

have grown used to thinking, in prosperity,

but in the development of the soul.

ALEXANDER SOLZHENITSYN
Awarded Nobel prize for literature, 1970

As the flower is before the fruit, so is faith

before good works.

RICHARD WHATLEY

The controversy about faith and works is one that has gone on for a very long time, and it is a highly technical matter. I personally rely on the paradoxical text: "Work out your own salvation...for it is God that worketh in you." It looks as if in one sense we do nothing, and in another case we do a [whole] lot. "Work out your own salvation with fear and trembling," but you must have it in you before your can work it out.

hat good is it, my brothers, if a man claims to have faith but has no deeds? Can such faith save him? Suppose a brother or sister is without clothes and daily food. If one of you says to him, "Go, I wish you well; keep warm and well fed," but does nothing about his physical needs, what good is it? In the same way, faith by itself, if it is not accompanied by action, is dead.

JAMES 2:14-17 NIV

BY FAITH WE KNOW
HIS EXISTENCE, IN
GLORY WE SHALL
KNOW HIS NATURE.

BLAISE PASCAL

Faith is the substance of things hoped for, the
evidence of things not seen.

HEBREWS 11:1 NKJV

Faith is the daring of the soul to go farther
than it can see.

Faith is for that which lies on the other side of
reason. Faith is what makes life bearable, with
all its tragedies and sudden, startling joys.

MADELEINE L'ENGLE

FAITH

For what is faith unless it is to believe
what you do not see?

ST. AUGUSTINE

Call it faith, call it vitality, call it the will to live,

call it the religion of tomorrow morning, call it

the immortality of man...it is the thing that

explains why man survives all things and why

there is no such thing as a pessimist.

G. K. CHESTERTON

I had spent my first 40 years seeking the whole world, to the neglect of my soul. But what I couldn't find in my quest for power and success—that is true security and meaning—I discovered in prison where all worldly props had been stripped away. And by God's grace, I lost my life in order that I might find true life in Christ....

Watergate caused my world to crash around me and sent me to prison. I lost many of the mainstays of my existence—the awards, the six-figure income and lifestyle to match, arguing cases in the highest courts, a position of power at the right hand of the President of the United States. But only when I lost them did I find a far greater gain: knowing Christ. I learned the truth of Jesus' words, "He who wishes to save his life shall lose it. But whoever loses his life for My sake shall find it." ❖

CHARLES COLSON
Special Counsel to President Richard Nixon and recipient of the 1993 Templeton Progress in Religion Award for work among prisoners.

God declares that calling on His name in a

despairing condition is a sure port of safety.

JOHN CALVIN

When it is dark enough, you can see the stars.

CHARLES A. BEARD

ou have more faith than you think you have. You have faith enough to pray; you have faith enough to believe that you will be heard.

OLE HALLESBY

If I find in myself a desire which no experience in this world can satisfy, the most probable explanation is that I was made for another world.

C. S. LEWIS

God has not made a little universe. He has made the wide stretches of space and has put there all the flaming hosts we see at night, all the planets, stars, and galaxies. Wherever we go let us remind ourselves that God has made everything we see…. And not only did God make it all, but He is present.

FRANCIS A. SCHAEFFER

Faith is building on what you know is here so you can reach what you know is there.

CULLEN HIGHTOWER

LIVING A LIFE OF FAITH MEANS
NEVER KNOWING WHERE YOU ARE
BEING LED. BUT IT DOES MEAN
LOVING AND KNOWING THE ONE
WHO IS LEADING. IT IS LITERALLY
A LIFE OF FAITH, NOT OF
UNDERSTANDING AND REASON—
A LIFE OF KNOWING HIM WHO
CALLS US TO GO.

OSWALD CHAMBERS

If you want to get warm you must stand near the fire: if you want to be wet you must get into water. If you want joy, power, peace, eternal life, you must get close to, or even into, the thing that has them. They are not a sort of prize which God could, if He chose, just hand out to anyone. They are a great fountain of energy and beauty spurting up at the very center of reality. If you are close to it, the spray will wet you: if you are not, you will remain dry. Once a man is united to God, how could he not live forever?

C. S. LEWIS

W hat a tremendous relief it should be, and has been to many, to discover that we don't need to prove ourselves to God. We don't have to do anything at all, to be acceptable to Him.... Jesus came to say, hey, you don't have to earn God's love. It is not a matter for human achievement. You exist because God loves you already.

DESMOND TUTU
Awarded Nobel prize for peace, 1984

F aith is like a boomerang; begin using what you have and it comes back to you in greater measure.

CHARLES ALLEN

I see Heaven's glories shine,
And faith shines equal,
  arming me from fear.

EMILY BRONTË

Ultimately, faith is the only key to the universe. The final meaning of human existence, and the answers to the questions on which all our happiness depends, cannot be found in any other way.

THOMAS MERTON

The final stage in the life of faith is attainment of character.

OSWALD CHAMBERS

Faith is simultaneously long perseverance and unwavering confidence.

PIERRE-YVES EMERY

The soul can split the sky in two,
And let the face of God shine through.

EDNA ST. VINCENT MILLAY

I said to the man who stood at the gate

of the year,

"Give me a light that I may tread safely

into the unknown."

And he replied, "Step out into the darkness,

Put your hand into the hand of God,

And that will be to you better than a light

And safer than a known way."

PHILIP HASBRO

More things are wrought by prayer

Than this world dreams of.

ALFRED, LORD TENNYSON

Faith in small things has repercussions

that ripple all the way out. In a huge, dark

room a little match can light up the place.

JONI EARECKSON TADA

Yes, he is a great favorite everywhere.

He is to be president of the United States some

day; if I had not thought so I never would have

married him, for you can see he is not pretty. But

look at him! Doesn't he look as if he would make

a magnificent President?

MARY TODD LINCOLN
Spoken about 15 years before it became true

FAITH IS NOT A SHELTER AGAINST DIFFICULTIES, BUT BELIEF IN THE FACE OF ALL CONTRADICTIONS.

PAUL TOURNIER

F aith, in the sense in which I am here

using the word, is the art of holding on

to things your reason has once accepted,

in spite of your changing moods. For moods will

change, whatever view your reason takes. I know

that by experience. Now that I am a Christian I

do have moods in which the whole thing looks

very improbable: but when I was an atheist I had

moods in which Christianity looked terribly

probable. This rebellion of your moods against your real self is going to come anyway. That is why Faith is such a necessary virtue: unless you teach your moods "where they get off," you can never be either a sound Christian or even a sound atheist, but just a creature dithering to and fro, with its beliefs really dependent on the weather and the state of its digestion.

C. S. LEWIS

O ptimism is the faith that
leads to achievement. Nothing
can be done without hope.

HELEN KELLER

H ope means to keep living
amid desperation
and to keep humming
in the darkness.

HENRI J. M. NOUWEN

'TIS NOT THE DYING FOR
A FAITH THAT'S SO HARD…
EVERY MAN OF EVERY NATION
HAS DONE THAT—'TIS
THE LIVING UP TO IT
THAT'S DIFFICULT.

WILLIAM MAKEPEACE THACKERAY

ALFRED, LORD TENNYSON
Crossing the Bar

Sunset and evening star,

And one clear call for me!

And may there be no moaning of the bar,

When I put out to sea,

But such a tide as moving seems asleep,

Too full for sound and foam,

When that which drew from out

the boundless deep

Turns again home.

Twilight and evening bell,

And after that the dark!

And may there be no sadness of farewell,

When I embark;

Crossing the bar

For though from out our bourne of Time

and Place

The flood may bear me far,

I hope to see my Pilot face-to-face

When I have cross'd the bar. ❖

Faith is a certitude without proofs.... Faith is
a sentiment, for it is a hope; it is an instinct,
for it precedes all outward instruction.

HENRI FRÉDÉRIC AMIEL

Faith is a cliff on which the weak wave breaks,

    The tree around whose mighty frail

        tendrils twine,

    In cloudy skies it sets a starry sign,

And in the sorrowing soul an altar makes.

THOMAS S. JONES

BE FAITHFUL IN LITTLE
THINGS, FOR IN THEM OUR
STRENGTH LIES. TO THE
GOOD GOD NOTHING IS
LITTLE, BECAUSE HE IS SO
GREAT AND WE SO SMALL.

MOTHER TERESA

The only faith that wears well and holds its color in all weather, is that which is woven of conviction and set with the sharp mordant of experience.

J. R. LOWELL

The principal part of faith is patience.

GEORGE MacDONALD

One does not discover new
lands without consenting
to lose sight of the shore.

ANDRÉ GIDE
Awarded Nobel prize for literature, 1947

God has not called me to be
successful; He has called me
to be faithful.

MOTHER TERESA

A nybody who has been seriously engaged in scientific work of any kind realizes that over the entrance to the gates of the temple of science are written the words: *Ye must have faith.* It is a quality which the scientist cannot dispense with.

MAX PLANCK

I have believed the best of every man,

And find that to believe it is enough

To make a bad man show him at his best,

Or even a good man swing his lantern higher.

WILLIAM BUTLER YEATS

F aith is an excitement and an enthusiasm: it is

a condition of intellectual magnificence to which

we must cling as to a treasure, and not squander.

GEORGE SAND

FAITH

73

Do not worry about your life,

what you will eat or drink;

or about your body,

what you will wear.

Is not life more important than food,

and the body more important than clothes?

Look at the birds of the air;

they do not sow or reap or store away in barns,

and yet your heavenly Father feeds them.

Are you not much more valuable than they?

MATTHEW 6:25,26 NIV

IT IS CYNICISM AND
FEAR THAT FREEZE
LIFE; IT IS FAITH
THAT THAWS IT
OUT, RELEASES IT,
SETS IT FREE.

HARRY EMERSON FOSDICK

I do not want merely to possess a faith,
I want a faith that possesses me.

CHARLES KINGSLEY

Faith always shows itself in the
whole personality.

MARTYN LLOYD-JONES

Faith declares what the senses do not
see, but not the contrary of what
they see. It is above them, not
contrary to them.

BLAISE PASCAL

Understanding is the reward of faith. Therefore seek not to understand that you may believe, but believe that you may understand.

ST. AUGUSTINE

Not only in actions but in faith also has God preserved man's free and unconstrained choice. He says, "Let it happen to you according to your faith," thus showing that faith is something which a man has as his own, just as he has his own power of decision.

IRENAEUS

JOYCE KILMER
Tree

I think that I shall never see

A poem lovely as a tree.

A tree whose hungry mouth is prest

Against the earth's sweet flowing breast;

A tree that looks at God all Day,

And lifts her leafy arms to pray;

A tree that may in Summer wear

A nest of robins in her hair;

Upon whose bosom snow has lain;

Who intimately lives with rain.

Poems are made by fools like me,

But only God can make a tree.

MARY PETERS

Through the love of God our Father

All will be well.

Free and changeless is His favor,

All will be well.

Precious is the blood that healed us,

Perfect is the grace that sealed us,

Strong the hand stretched out to shield us,

All will be well.

We expect a bright tomorrow,

All will be well.

Faith can sing through days of sorrow,

All will be well.

On our Father's love relying,

Jesus every need supplying

In our living, in our dying,

All will be well.

Never, never pin your whole faith on any human being: not if he is the best and wisest in the whole world. There are lots of nice things you can do with sand; but do not try building a house on it.

C. S. LEWIS

Jesus answered, "I am the way and the truth and the life."

JOHN 14:6 NIV

FAITH

82

STEP OUT IN FAITH!

JOHANN SEBASTIAN BACH

ow faith is being sure of what we hope for and certain of what we do not see. This is what the ancients were commended for. By faith we understand that the universe was formed at God's command, so that what is seen was not made out of what was visible.... And without faith it is impossible to please God, because anyone who comes to him must believe that he exists and that he rewards those who earnestly seek him.

HEBREWS 11:1-3,6 NIV

Belief is truth held in the mind;

faith is a fire in the heart.

JOSEPH FORT NEWTON

Faith is not an effort, a striving, a ceaseless

seeking, as so many earnest souls suppose, but

rather a letting go, an abandonment, an abiding

rest in God that nothing, not even the soul's

shortcomings, can disturb.

here can I go from your Spirit?
Where can I flee from your presence?
If I go up to the heavens, you are there;
    if I make my bed in the depths, you are there.
If I rise on the wings of the dawn,
    if I settle on the far side of the sea,
even there your hand will guide me,
    your right hand will hold me fast.

If I say, "Surely the darkness will hide me
    and the light become night around me,"
even the darkness will not be dark to you;
    the night will shine like the day,
    for darkness is as light to you.

For you created my inmost being;
    you knit me together in my mother's womb.

FAITH

86

I praise you because I am fearfully and
      wonderfully made;
   your works are wonderful,
   I know that full well.
My frame was not hidden from you
   when I was made in the secret place.

When I was woven together in the depths
      of the earth,
   your eyes saw my unformed body.
All the days ordained for me
   were written in your book
   before one of them came to be....

Search me, O God, and know my heart.

PSALM 139:7-16,23 NIV